T0083064

DAVID BEDNALL

MAKE WE MERRY

SSAA and organ (with optional brass)

David Bednall

Contents

1. Make we merry 2
2. The time draws near 6
3. The Christ-child lay on Mary's lap 11
4. All this night shrill chanticleer 14
5. Moonless darkness stands between 20
6. Sweet was the song 24
7. Let others look for pearl and gold 27
8. Make we joy now 31

Duration: 25 minutes

An accompaniment for brass ensemble, organ, and percussion is available on hire/rental from the publisher or appropriate agent. For performances with brass, the organ part available on hire/rental should be used, rather than the part in the vocal score.

MUSIC DEPARTMENT

OXFORD
UNIVERSITY PRESS

for Edward Whiting and Benenden Chapel Choir
and with grateful thanks to Julian Metherell for his kind and generous support

Make We Merry

DAVID BEDNALL

1. Make we merry

Anon. *c.*1500

© Oxford University Press 2019

Printed in Great Britain

OXFORD UNIVERSITY PRESS, MUSIC DEPARTMENT, GREAT CLARENDON STREET, OXFORD OX2 6DP
The Moral Rights of the Composer have been asserted. Photocopying this copyright material is ILLEGAL.

14
f
For now is the time, now is the time, now is the time of Chri - ste - mas!
Ped.
f
19
f
Let no man_ come in - to this hall, Nor
mf
Man.
24
groom, nor page, nor yet mar - shall, But that some sport he bring with all.
ff
Make_ we mer-ry both
f
29
more and less,
mf
For now is the time, now is the time,
mf
Ped.

34
ff
now is the time of Chri - ste - mas!
f
mf legato
p
Man.
39
mp cantabile
mf
If he say that he can - not sing, Some o - ther sport then let him bring, That it may please at this feast - ing.
mf
Ped.
45
mp
Make we mer-ry, make we mer-ry, make we mer-ry, both more and less.
mp
p
49
p
mf
If he say naught can he do, Then,

54
f
ffp
molto
for my love, tell him no, But to the stocks then let him go.
mp
mf
f
59
fff
S.
Mer - ry, mer - ry, make we now mer-ry both more and less, make we mer-ry,
fff
A.
Make we mer-ry, make we mer-ry, make we now mer-ry both more and less, make we mer-ry,
ff
64
f
ff
fff
make we mer-ry, for now is the time, now is the time, now is the time of Chri - ste - mas!
f
ff
fff
make we mer-ry, for now is the time, now is the time, now is the time of Chri - ste - mas!
f
ff

2. *The time draws near*

Alfred, Lord Tennyson (1809–92)

© Oxford University Press 2019. Photocopying this copyright material is ILLEGAL.

25
mp
Four voi - ces of four ham - lets round, From far and near, on mead and moor,
Man.
30
S.
mf
Swell out and fail, as if a door Were shut be-tween me and the sound.
A.
mf
Swell out and fail, as if a door Were shut be-tween me and the sound.
Gt.
mp
35
mp
Each voice four
mp
Each voice four
Gt.
mp

41
mf
mp
chan - ges on the wind, That now di - late, and now de - crease,
mf
mp
chan - ges on the wind, That now di - late, and now de - crease,
47
mf ma molto dolce
Peace and good - will, good - will and peace, Peace and good - will to all man - kind.
mf ma molto dolce
Peace and good - will, good - will and peace, Peace and good - will to all man - kind.
mp sonore
Ped.
55
S./A.
unis. mp
This
p
pp

61
A little faster ♩ = c.84
mf
year I slept and woke with pain, I al-most wished no more to wake, And that my
mp
66
molto f
hold on life would break Be-fore I heard those bells a-
molto f
hold on life would break Be-fore I heard those bells, those
f sonore
72
ff ma dolce
-gain: But they my trou-bled spi-rit rule,
ff ma dolce
bells a-gain: But they my trou-bled spi-rit rule,

77
mf sonore
rit.
For they con - trolled me when a boy; They bring me sor - row touched with joy,
mf sonore
For they con - trolled me when a boy; They bring me sor - row touched with joy,
rit.
mf
82
Tempo I
mp
S. 1
The mer - ry bells of Yule, the mer - ry bells of Yule,
mp
S. 2
The mer - ry bells of Yule, the mer - ry bells of
mp
A.
The mer - ry bells, the mer - ry
Tempo I
mp
87
p
pp
ppp
bells of Yule.
p
pp
ppp
Yule, of Yule.
p
pp
ppp
bells, bells of Yule.
p
ppp
ppp

3. The Christ-child lay on Mary's lap

G. K. Chesterton (1874–1936)

13
mf
hair was like a star. (O stern and cun-ning are the kings, But
mf
hair was like a star. (O stern and cun - ning are the kings, But
mf
17
mp
p
teneramente
here the true hearts are.) The Christ - child lay on Ma - ry's heart,
mp
p
teneramente
here the true hearts are.) The Christ - child lay on Ma - ry's, Ma - ry's
mp
p
21
molto f ma dolce
His hair, his hair was like a fire, like a fire. (O
molto f ma dolce
heart, His hair, his hair was like a fire, like a fire. (O
f

25
mf
mp
wea - ry, wea - ry is the world, But here the world's de - sire.) The
wea - ry, wea - ry is the world, But here the world's de - sire.) The
29
mf
mp but very warm
Christ - child stood at Ma - ry's knee, His hair was like a crown, And
Christ - child stood at Ma - ry's knee, His hair was like a crown, And
Ped.
33
p
pp
all the flowers looked up at him, And all the stars looked down.
all the flowers looked up at him, And all the stars looked down.

4. *All this night shrill chanticleer*

William Austin (1587–1634)

© Oxford University Press 2019. Photocopying this copyright material is ILLEGAL.

14
f
Claps his wings and loud - ly cries, claps his wings and loud - ly cries,
f
Claps his wings and loud - ly cries, claps his wings and loud - ly cries,
Gt.
f
18
ff
fff
'Mor - tals, mor - tals, wake and rise!
ff
fff
'Mor - tals, mor - tals, wake and rise!
ff
f
23
unis.
f
See a won - der Hea - ven is un - der,
27
mf
f
ff
S.
A.
From the earth is ris'n a Sun Shines all night though day be done.
mf
ff

31
S.
f cantabile
Wake, O earth, wake ev - 'ry -
A.
f cantabile
Wake, O earth,
mf
Man.
35
- thing, Wake and hear the joy I bring, Wake and joy,
wake ev - 'ry - thing, Wake and hear the joy I bring, Wake and joy,
Ped.
39
ff
mf
wake and joy, wake and joy; for all this
ff
mf
wake and joy, wake and joy; for all this
ff
f
mf
Man.

44
night Hea - ven and ev - 'ry twink-ling light, All a - maz - ing,
night Hea - ven and ev - 'ry twink-ling light, All a - maz - ing,
f
Ped.
49
Still stand gaz - ing, An - gels, pow - ers and all that be,
Still stand gaz - ing, An - gels, pow - ers and all that be,
ff
ff molto sonore
55
Wake and joy this Sun, this Sun to see.
Wake and joy this Sun, this Sun to see.
mf

61
cresc.
65
ff
fff
ff
Hail, O Sun, O bless - ed Light, Sent in - to the world by night,
Hail, O Sun, O bless - ed Light, Sent in - to the world by night,
ff
f
Man.
Ped.
Man.
Ped.
69
f
mf
Let thy rays and heav'n-ly pow - ers Shine in this dark soul of ours;
Let thy rays and heav'n-ly pow - ers Shine in this dark soul of ours;
mf

73
f
ff
For most du - ly Thou art tru - ly God and
For most du - ly Thou art tru - ly God and
78
mf
f
man we do con - fess. Hail, O Sun, hail, O
man we do con - fess. Hail, O Sun, hail, O
83
ff
fff
Sun, hail, Sun of Right - - eous-ness!'
Sun, hail, Sun of Right - - eous-ness!'

5. *Moonless darkness stands between*

Gerard Manley Hopkins (1844–99)

© Oxford University Press 2019. Photocopying this copyright material is ILLEGAL.

18
mf
Past, the past, no more be seen!
p
mf
Past, the past, no more be seen!
p
mf
p
mp
Ped.
23
mp
But the Beth - le - hem - star may lead me To the
mp
But the Beth - le - hem - star may lead me To the
28
mf
sight of him who freed me From the
mf
sight of him, of him who freed me From the
mf

32
f dolce
self that I have been.
Make me pure, Lord:
p
f dolce
self that I have been.
Make me pure, Lord:
p
f dolce
mp
Man.
p
Ped.
38
thou art ho - ly;
Make me meek, Lord:
thou art ho - ly;
Make me meek, Lord:
43
f dolce
thou wert low - ly;
Now be - gin - ning,
f dolce
thou wert low - ly;
Now be - gin - ning,
f sonore

47
and al - way: Now be - gin on Christ - mas day.
and al - way: Now be - gin on Christ - mas day.
52
p
Moon - less dark-ness stands be - tween.
p
Moon - less dark-ness stands be - tween.
p
Man.
rit.
56
mf
p
ppp
Past, the past, no more be seen!
mf
p
ppp
Past, the past, no more be seen!
rit.
mf
p
ppp
Ped.

6. *Sweet was the song*

from William Ballet's Lute Book (16th cent.)

* pronounce as *loo-la*

© Oxford University Press 2019. Photocopying this copyright material is ILLEGAL.

19
mp
mf
on her knee.
'Sweet babe,' quoth she, 'My
mp
mp
Man.
25
poco f
son, And eke a Sa-viour born, Who hast vouch-safed from on high To
mf
29
mp
vi - sit us that were for-lorn.'
Lul - la, lul - la, lul - la, lul-la-by,
mp
34
p
poco rit.
a tempo
p teneramente
lul - la, lul - la-by.
Sweet was the song the Vir-gin sang, When
p
pp
Ped.

39
she to Beth - lem Ju-da came And was de-li-vered of a Son That bless - ed Je-sus hath to
44
S.
name. Lul - la, lul - la, lul - la, lul-la-by, lul - la, lul-la-by. 'Sweet babe,' quoth
p
poco f
A.
name. Lul - la, lul - la, lul - la, lul-la-by, lul - la, lul-la-by. 'Sweet
p
poco f
p
mf
50
she, And rocked him sweet-ly on her knee.
mf
mp
p
pp
rit.
babe,' quoth she, And rocked him sweet-ly on her knee.
mf
mp
p
pp
rit.
mp
dolce
pp
ppp

7. Let others look for pearl and gold

Robert Herrick (1591–1674)

* May be used in performance if necessary
† *tabbies* = silk taffetas

© Oxford University Press 2019. Photocopying this copyright material is ILLEGAL.

7
f molto dolce
mp
hay Where-on the bless - ed ba - by lay, Or one poor swad - dling
hay Where-on the bless - ed, the bless - ed ba - by lay, Or one poor swad - dling
hay Where-on the bless - - ed, the bless - ed ba - by lay, Or one poor swad - dling
hay Where-on the bless - ed, bless - ed ba - by lay, Or one poor swad - dling
10
mf
poco rit.
a tempo
p
poco
clout,* shall be The rich - est New-Year's gift to me. Let o-thers look for pearl and
clout,*shall be The rich - est, rich-est New-Year's gift to me. Let o-thers look for pearl and
clout,*shall be The rich - est, rich-est New-Year's gift to me. Let o-thers look for pearl and
clout,*shall be The rich - est, rich-est New-Year's gift to me. Let o-thers look for pearl and

* *clout* = cloth

14
mp
mf
gold, for pearl and gold, Tis-sues, or tab - bies ma - ni - fold:
gold, for pearl and gold, Tis - sues, or tab-bies ma - ni - fold:
gold, for pearl and gold, Tis - sues, or tab - bies ma - ni-fold:
gold, for pearl and gold, Tis - sues, or tab-bies ma - ni-fold:
18
p
f molto dolce
One on - ly lock of that sweet hay Where-on the bless - ed ba - by lay,
One on - ly lock of that sweet hay Where-on the bless - ed, the bless - ed ba - by lay,
One on - ly lock of that sweet hay Where-on the bless - ed, the bless - ed ba - by lay,
One on - ly lock of that sweet hay Where-on the bless - ed, bless - ed ba - by lay,

21
mf
molto f ma dolce
Or one poor swad - dling clout, shall be The rich - - - est
Or one poor swad - dling clout, shall be The rich - est gift, rich - est
Or one poor swad - dling clout, shall be The rich - est gift, rich - est
Or one poor swad - dling clout, shall be The rich - est gift, rich - est

rit.
24
mf
pp
gift, shall be The rich-est gift, The rich-est New-Year's gift to me.
gift, shall be The rich-est gift, The rich-est New - Year's gift to me.
gift, shall be The rich-est gift, The rich-est New - Year's gift to me.
gift, shall be The rich-est gift, The rich-est New - Year's gift to me.

8. Make we joy now

Anon 15th cent.

[1] In which Christ is born

© Oxford University Press 2019. Photocopying this copyright material is ILLEGAL.

[2] The Only-begotten of the Father

[3] Come, Redeemer of the nations

[4] Let every age perceive (that)

[5] The high Word forthcoming [6] From the rising of the sun

7 Which our father Adam defiled

[8] Mary conceived in her womb [9] Sharing in the light of his Father

[10] O Light of the Holy Trinity

[11] Glory to thee, O Lord!

Music originated by Andrew Jones
Printed in England by Halstan & Co. Ltd, Amersham, Bucks.